Hand in Hand
with God

Hand in Hand *with* God

A Collection of Life-giving Poetry by Mary Dreisbach

© 2010 by Mary Dreisbach. All rights reserved.

Pleasant Word (a division of WinePress Publishing, PO Box 428, Enumclaw, WA 98022) functions only as book publisher. As such, the ultimate design, content, editorial accuracy, and views expressed or implied in this work are those of the author.

No part of this publication may be reproduced, stored in a retrieval system, or transmitted in any way by any means—electronic, mechanical, photocopy, recording, or otherwise—without the prior permission of the copyright holder, except as provided by USA copyright law.

Unless otherwise noted, all Scriptures are taken from the *Holy Bible, New International Version®, NIV®*. Copyright © 1973, 1978, 1984 by Biblica, Inc.™ Used by permission of Zondervan. All rights reserved worldwide. WWW.ZONDERVAN.COM

Scripture references marked NKJV are taken from the *New King James Version* of the Bible. Copyright © 1982 by Thomas Nelson, Inc. Used by permission. All rights reserved.

Scripture references marked NLT are taken from the *New Living Translation* of the Bible. Copyright © 1996, 2004 by Tyndale Charitable Trust. Used by permission of Tyndale House Publishers.

ISBN 13: 978-1-4141-1669-3
ISBN 10: 1-4141-1669-1
Library of Congress Catalog Card Number: 2009943257

This book is dedicated to Jesus Christ, my Savior, Redeemer, and Lord over my life, who has taken me by the hand and rescued me from the pit time and time again. It is He who gives me the courage to write and walks alongside me through life. It is with a heart full of gratitude and praise for Him that I share these words with you.

I also dedicate this book to all those who find themselves in a dark place, a broken place, a helpless place, or an enslaved place. Though they cannot change your circumstances, these poems are written for you, to help you find encouragement, hope, and peace that can only be found in Jesus. Reach out your hand, Jesus is waiting for you. Take His hand and don't let go. He is there, He is waiting, He is patient, and He loves you.

Contents

Introduction xi
Hand in Hand with God 1
On My Knees 3
The Rescuer 4
Out of the Darkness, into the Light 5
Mysterious 7
Hanging On 8
Distant 9
Strength in Him 11
I Am Your God . . . Your Hope 12
In Him 14
Secure in Him 16
More than a Conqueror 17
Be Still and Know that I am God 20
Serve God 22
Patient Lord 23
Tear Catcher 25
Grateful Tears 27
I Belong 28
Joy of the Lord 29
Deliverance 30
Because I Prayed 31
Divine Connection 32
God's Love 34

Faithful, Loving Father 36
Marking the Trail 38
Why Do I Run from You, Lord?. 39
When I Fall 40
Empty Canvas 41
God's Truth 43
Worry. 44
Slow Down 46
Keep Him in the Center of Your Day. 48
Living for the Lord. 50
Lord, I Just Want to be Happy. 52
All for You Today 54
Morning Routine 55
God's Armor 57
Thinking Differently 59
What Do You Think?. 61
Our Days. 62
The Opposite Practice 64
Can You Still Use Me Broken? 66
If I Could Be 68
Trouble in this Life. 70
Jesus in Me. 72
Walking in His Way. 73
The Inheritance 74
The Journey 76
Home Sweet Home 78
Heaven Bound. 80
Heaven. 82
Life Reflections. 85

The Junk Drawer 86
Send Your Peace 88
Questions, Lord? 89
The Woman at the Well 90
Jesus Came 93
Matchless Love 95
His Scars 97
For You and for Me 99
Lay it All Down 101
Victory 102
RSVP 104
GPS (God's Positioning System) 105
God's Plan For Me 106
Eternal Perspective 107
Praise to God 109
The Message 111
Shout Out Your Song 113
All for You, Jesus 115
Shepherd and Sheep 116
Bunnies 118
Meet Me There 120
Look Around 122
Creation's Gift 124
The Living Masterpiece 126

Introduction

Hand in Hand with God is a collection of poems inspired by my own personal journey in discovering the comfort, security, love, and power we have through the grace and promises of God. There are amazing benefits afforded us as God's children if we are willing to place our hand in His and walk the road of life with Him by our side.

I am just an ordinary woman living out an extraordinary life. I am held firmly by the strength of God's hand. He is a God who loves me, knows me, and will never let me go.

These poems were born in moments of walking hand in hand with God. They are meant to inspire, encourage, and draw you closer to our great and loving God. I pray that as you read, you will find new ways to grab hold of His outstretched hand and cultivate your own relationship with Jesus, our Life Giver, and the Lover of our souls.

If the LORD delights in a man's way, he makes his steps firm; though he stumble, he will not fall, for the LORD upholds him with his hand. I was young and now I am old, yet I have never seen the righteous forsaken or their children begging bread.
—Ps. 37:23-25

Yet I am always with you; you hold me by my right hand.
—Psa. 73:23

You will be a crown of splendor in the Lord's hand, a royal diadem in the hand of your God.
—Isa. 62:3

That is why, for Christ's sake, I delight in weaknesses, in insults, in hardships, in persecutions, in difficulties. For when I am weak, then I am strong.

—2 Cor. 12:10

Hand in Hand with God

Wandering in desolation,
Hopeless with despair,
Couldn't see through darkness,
Caught in evil's snare.

Entangled by the lies,
Coiled up in sin,
Engulfed by sheer deception,
Advancing for the win.

I call out to my God,
Reaching toward the sky.
God puts His hand in mine,
Quieting my cry.

God sees me in my weakest state,
Renews me with His strength,
Reclaims the land I've lost to sin,
He goes to every length.

Assures my life in Him's restored,
That I may rest secure,
Beneath the shelter of His wings,
Till I can once more soar.

Hand in Hand with God

He leads me by still waters.
Walking hand in hand,
He gently helps untangle sin,
Helping me to stand.

I thank You God, that when I'm weak,
I find my strength in You.
Your loving hand sustains me
In all I'm going through.

My soul yearns, even faints, for the courts of the LORD; my heart and my flesh cry out for the living God.
—Ps. 84:2

On My Knees

Here I am, Lord,
On my knees,
Hands outstretched,
Crying out,
Desiring more of You.

Pour into me Your Spirit, Lord.
Fill me up to overflowing.
I surrender all I am
For You to use.

Take me and make me
Into what you'll have me be.
Empty all the garbage
From my heart.

Erase the fear,
The pride, and shame,
Replacing them with
Love's bright flame;
Igniting a fresh fire deep within.

"Because he loves me," says the LORD, "I will rescue him; I will protect him, for he acknowledges my name."

—Ps. 91:14

The Rescuer

Shelter from the storm,
Resting in His arms.
He lifts me high upon the rock,
Rescues me from harm.
Covers me in love, enables me to stand
Firm and strong in truth, steadied by His hand.

When I falter in my steps,
He always calls me back;
He never lets me fall beyond His reach.
He's given me this gift
Of His unfailing love,
Sacrificing all He has for me.

My sin was washed away
By the shedding of His blood.
His mercy and His grace are given free.
I praise You, mighty God,
For the wonders of Your love.
And thank You for all You've done for me.

Praise be to the God and Father of our Lord Jesus Christ, the Father of compassion and the God of all comfort, who comforts us in all our troubles, so that we can comfort those in any trouble with the comfort we ourselves have received from God.
—2 Cor. 1:3-4

For you were once darkness, but now you are light in the Lord. Live as children of light.
—Eph. 5:8

Out of the Darkness, into the Light

These scars bear testimony to the thrashing that took place
Within the workings of my soul when the darkness hid Your face.

Afraid, rejected, shamed, alone, wishing I were dead
There were no happy moments; only pain, despair, and dread.

Bound and trapped by heavy chains wrapped around my feet,
There was nowhere I could go, captivity complete.

I lay there on the bottom of that filthy, slimy pit.
All energy had drained away, all I wanted was to quit.

I sent a cry into the air, hoping it would reach God's ear.
My only chance at rescue, I started praying He would hear.

In the silence of the darkness, though unable to see,
I felt somebody take my hand. He said, "I'm here to set you free."

Hand in Hand with God

"I heard your cry, my precious child, you've suffered far too long.
Now let me lift you out of here, I'll fix you up and make you strong."

God placed me on His shoulders, as He began the climb,
The light before me brightened as we left the dark behind.

The hopeless, desperate feelings weren't as scary in the light.
God took them and replaced them with a newfound will to fight.

As a toddler takes first steps, I wobbled and fell down.
The more I placed my trust in God, I knew He wouldn't let me drown.

With every movement forward, my faith and confidence soared.
I answered every knocking, as I opened up the door.

In my weakness God remade me daughter of the King,
Now my heart and soul cry out, and thankfulness I sing!

Though scars of past hurts still remain, they are not who I am.
God used me and the pain I felt to advance His kingdom plan.

Not only so, but we also rejoice in our sufferings, because we know that suffering produces perseverance; perseverance, character; and character, hope.
—Rom. 5:3-4

Mysterious

Can we appreciate true wholeness, unless we've traveled through the broken?
In never hearing harsh words, will we hear those gently spoken?

Can we savor warming sunshine, if we've never been through rain?
If we've never known the depth of loss, can we ever know real gain?

It is in going through the chaos that true peace can be found.
And weeping in great sorrow that gives way to blissful sound.

Having never known depression may seem a gift to some.
But in the depth of heaviness, strength in Him will come.

In the midst of grieving, we may shed so many tears;
But it is through that revelation that His great love will appear.

God uses every evil, tragedy, and pain
To lift us up out of the pit, back on our feet again.

If we'd have never fallen, would we take standing up for granted?
If we've never been uprooted, can we cherish being planted?

Having never walked in darkness, can we appreciate the light?
God gives these opportunities for growing day and night.

In all life's situations, there's a lesson to be learned.
Pay attention to God's movement, so His truth can be discerned.

For sin shall not be your master, because you are not under law, but under grace.

—Rom. 6:14

Hanging On

Hanging on
Checking in
Going crazy
Lost in sin
Come quick
Save me.
Feel sick
Can't you see?
Thoughts race
All day.
God's grace
On the way.
Thanks, Lord,
Please forgive.
Your Word
Helps me live.
Fill my heart
With love
Never to part
With God above.
Hanging on
Checking in
No longer
Lost in sin.

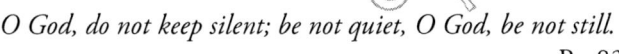

O God, do not keep silent; be not quiet, O God, be not still.
—Ps. 83:1

Distant

God, where are you?
Strong Tower
Rock
Deliverer.

Where do You hide?
My Father
Protector
Redeemer.

Why so silent?
Whisper
Breathe
Anything.

Just so I know . . .
You're present
Here
Loving me.

*"It's you who's been so distant child . . .
Come
Sit
Embrace."*

Hand in Hand with God

Ashamed,
I humbly
Seek
Your face.

Forgiving, loving God
Generous
Full
Of grace.

The Lord is my rock, my fortress and my deliverer; my God is my rock, in whom I take refuge. He is my shield and the horn of my salvation, my stronghold.

—Ps. 18:2

Strength in Him

My Rock, my Rock, deliver me.
Lift me high above my enemies.
Most wonderful and awesome God,
Your mighty hand picks me up.
You cradle me in Your strong arms.
You stand beside me through the battle.
This war has been waged against my will,
But I will not run.
I will stand in You and You in me.
Together united.
My enemy will seek me out.
He will pursue me with a vengeance,
Try to devour me,
Tempt me to turn from You, oh, Lord;
But you are my stronghold.
Your foundation of faithfulness will see me through.
Your love beyond all understanding
Gives me the courage to push on,
Not to give up.
My triumph is in You, oh, Lord.
Your peacefulness encompasses my spirit.
The wisdom in Your Word soothes my mind.
With Your breath upon me
I can soar like an eagle above the storms of this world,
And rest gently in your arms tonight.
I love you!
Amen.

Find rest, O my soul, in God alone; my hope comes from him. He alone is my rock and my salvation; he is my fortress, I will not be shaken.

—Ps. 62:5-6

I Am Your God . . . Your Hope

When your hope is fading in the wind,
And you think you're near the end,
I gently whisper in your ear,
"On Me you can depend.

"I'm here for you, my child.
I've called you by your name.
Let Me calm your troubled heart
For this is why I came.

"You are wonderfully created,
Crafted by My hand.
I know every hair upon your head,
And I will help you stand.

"My love for you is perfect.
I will restore your hope.
For it is I who lifts you up
And helps your mind to cope.

"I've searched your heavy heart.
I know your every thought.
Now lay your burdens at My feet;

I Am Your God . . . Your Hope

The battle has been fought."

"Take refuge in My promise.
Be encouraged by My Word.
Commit it to your memory.
Take hold the Spirit's sword.

"Put on the belt of truth,
To avoid the devil's charm;
The breastplate of My righteousness
To keep your heart from harm.

"Fit your feet with readiness,
The gospel of My peace.
Put on the helmet of salvation
So your thoughts of Me increase.

"With shooting fiery arrows
The evil one takes aim,
But your shield of faith is ready
To extinguish every flame.

"I've given you this armor,
Protection in the night.
Equipped you for your every need
So you can stand and fight.

"So when you feel hope fading,
Go put your armor on;
And pray to Me with all your might
Till the enemy has gone."

Trust in the Lord with all your heart and lean not on your own understanding; in all your ways acknowledge him, and he will make your paths straight.

—Prov. 3:5-6

In Him

Trust in the Lord with all your heart.
Do not be led astray.
He's been with you from the start.
Abide in Him today.

It's in the center of His will
That true peace can be found.
Sit before Him and be still,
He'll loose what has been bound.

Give Him all that's on your plate,
Don't try to take it back.
In Him sufficiency is great,
And nothing will you lack.

Be faithful to His holy Word.
Meditate upon its truth.
Practice all the things you've heard.
You'll surely make it through.

Hold tight to Him, this life is tough,
Let trust and faith not waver.
For He will *always* be enough.
Rest securely in His favor.

In Him

Love the Lord Your God
With all your heart, mind, and soul.
He'll guide you with His staff and rod
To your eternal goal.

His blood's been shed for you and me.
Sin's curse has been broken.
The sacrifice on Calvary
Was where the cry of love was spoken.

Praise the Lord throughout each day.
Remember what He's done.
Give thanks for all He's brought your way.
The victory He's won.

So trust the Lord with all you've got.
Give your life into His hands.
He'll always foil Satan's plot
When in Him you stand.

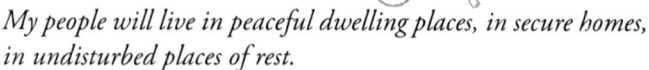

My people will live in peaceful dwelling places, in secure homes, in undisturbed places of rest.

—Isa. 32:18

Secure in Him

The gentle touch of Your hand upon my face
Sends shivers to the depths of my being
You whisper softly in my ear,
"I love you, my child,
Never fear."

Strong arms embrace me in the dark of night.
I'm safe and secure, resting in You.
I close my eyes and smile,
Drifting off in sleep
For a little while.

You have lifted me up on the highest rock.
Out of reach, standing, I come to realize
In You there's victory.
No enemy can
Reach me.

All will know that You are the Almighty God
When, with confidence, I stand before
The enemy of my soul,
Living life abundantly
For the eternal goal.

Let us then approach the throne of grace with confidence, so that we may receive mercy and find grace to help us in our time of need.
—Heb. 4:16

In all things we are more than conquerors through Him who loves us. For I am convinced that neither death nor life, neither angels or demons, neither the present nor the future, nor any powers, neither height nor depth, nor anything else in all creation. Will be able to separate us from the love of God that is in Christ Jesus our Lord.
—Rom. 8:37-39

More than a Conqueror

Past and present come together,
Clashing when they meet.
Warriors at battle,
Control is what they seek.

The common ground they prey on,
Is me, myself, and I.
Memories are their weapon,
The ammunition is their lies.

They penetrate the walls I've built,
Crushing my defenses,
Dredging up emotions
From all life's past offenses.

Shame and fear, guilt and hurt,
Cut through like a knife.
Feelings of abandonment
Felt throughout my life.

Hand in Hand with God

They haunt me and they taunt me,
Making me feel small.
Devouring my confidence,
Overtaken by them all.

But somewhere in the middle
Of this unrelenting war,
The tables turned and God stepped in,
Bringing courage to endure.

He strengthened my resistance.
He tended to my wounds.
Set me firmly on my feet,
So the battle could resume.

"You will overcome, my child.
Use Me as your shield.
In Me you are a conqueror
To whom the enemy will yield."

"Know that I am with you.
My love is all you need,
To make your past a footstool
And your present new in Me."

"I will guide you through the aftermath
And make your future bright.
Surrender all you are to Me
Walk boldly in My light."

More than a Conqueror

"My throne of grace awaits you.
Grace and mercy you'll receive.
Approach it with the confidence
That I'll supply your needs."

"Let your faith be an example
For all the world to see.
I will redeem all of your sufferings.
In Me your life's complete."

Be still, and know that I am God; I will be exalted among the nations, I will be exalted in the earth.

—Ps. 46:10

Be Still and Know that I am God

Be still and know that I am God
Come sit in My presence and see.
Pour out your heart before Me.
In the silence, there I'll be.

Let your mind come into focus.
I'll clear all your troubles away.
Release all the stress of your day
Into My hands as you pray.

In the calm of the moment I'll whisper
My life giving truth in your ear.
Replacing the lies that you fear
Healing as I hold you near.

I'm the God of past, present, and future
Every minute of time I am there.
I am with you everywhere,
I will show you how much I care.

Come to Me when you are weary,
I will give you the rest that you need,
Planting within you a seed
That will grow as you follow My lead.

Be Still and Know that I am God

Place your whole trust in Me.
Put your life into My hands.
I will help you to understand
As you live by My commands.

In this life you will have many trials,
Your faith will be put to the test.
Keep your eyes on Me in life's quest,
And you'll be eternally blessed.

I am your God and I love you.
Call out to Me when you are down.
I will lift you off of the ground,
Replace your suffering with a crown.

So come, child, get to know Me.
Sit with Me every day.
Listen for what I say
As you come into My presence to pray.

You will surely not be disappointed.
I'll reveal all that you need to know,
Causing your faith to grow.
Through you My love will flow.

Be still and know that I am God,
As you sit in My presence, you'll see.
I will speak to you ever so gently
The words that will set you free.

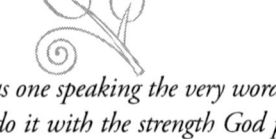

If anyone speaks, he should do it as one speaking the very words of God. If anyone serves, he should do it with the strength God provides, so that in all things God may be praised through Jesus Christ. To him be the glory and the power for ever and ever. Amen.
—1 Peter 4:11

Serve God

What can I do to serve You, Lord?
Please show me the way.
Fill me with Your Spirit
So Your glory is displayed.

Use me for Your purpose
In whatever capacity that may be.
Conform my will to Yours, Lord,
Take the focus off of me.

Let me be Your vessel,
The tool in Your hand.
Place me where I need to be
To complete what You have planned.

Help me to remember, Lord,
That I owe my life to You.
And that whose I am is evident
In all I say and do.

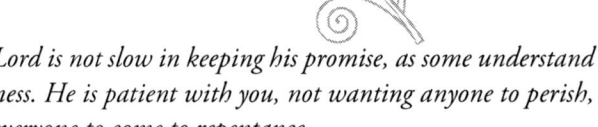

The Lord is not slow in keeping his promise, as some understand slowness. He is patient with you, not wanting anyone to perish, but everyone to come to repentance.

—2 Peter 3:9

Patient Lord

What is it that I can do for You,
My ever patient Lord?
You wait for me to come around
To take You at Your word.

You've laid out all Your promises
Before my very eyes.
You call me to take hold of them,
Letting go of Satan's lies.

I want to serve You with my life,
The life You've given me.
I want to give it back to You
Please shape it as You'll have me be.

Help me to let go, Lord,
Of the things I'm hanging onto.
Anything that comes between us,
Hindering what You want for me to do.

Take my hands, my feet, my mouth;
Take my eyes, my heart, my mind.
Use them for Your purposes,
Leaving my own self far behind.

Hand in Hand with God

I lay myself before You, Lord,
Empty, sinful, broken.
You can fill, forgive, and fix me
With the words of life You've spoken.

May my life become Your vessel
Filled to overflowing.
Spilling out Your testimony
Keeping all Your faithful growing.

It's my honor and my privilege
To be counted as Your own.
I give You all my praise and worship
Till the day You call me home!

You keep track of all my sorrows. You have collected all my tears in your bottle. You have recorded each one in your book.
—Ps. 56:8 (NLT)

Tear Catcher

Many kinds of tears are shed,
Tears of sorrow, tears of dread,
Tears that saturate our bed,
And those that stay tucked in our head.

Tears that trickle, tears that gush,
Tears that turn our hearts to mush,
Tears of embarrassment that make us flush,
Anxious tears when in a rush.

All these tears have wet our face.
Each one has its special place,
But today these tears, filled with God's grace
Come flowing at a frantic pace.

The realization of what He's done
For you, for me, for everyone.
Placing our sin on His only Son
Who willingly took it, so the battle was won.

Then sending His Spirit to guide our way,
To be with us night and day.
Flowing tears of thanks convey
The grateful hearts we now display.

Hand in Hand with God

The special meaning of each tear
Is something that our Lord holds dear.
Collecting them, He's always near,
Using what He's caught to wash away our fear.

Then very gently, He wipes us dry,
Lifting our faces to the sky.
On Him, we learn, we must rely
Each time we have ourselves a cry.

Those who sow in tears will reap with songs of joy.
—Ps. 126:5

Grateful Tears

Tears welled up from deep within
This grateful heart of mine.
One escaped, flowing down my face
In a single joyous line.

I caught it in a crystal glass,
And froze my tear of thanks
To give to You in appreciation
For going to such great lengths.

Sharing in my journey,
Helping me to grow,
Stretching my thought processes
In things I didn't know.

Of all the tears I've ever shed
This one I shan't forget.
The attitude of gratitude
In my heart for You is set.

Thank You for Your guidance.
Thank You for Your care.
I thank You with this tear of joy,
For the gifts You chose to share.

And provide for those who grieve in Zion—to bestow on them a crown of beauty instead of ashes, the oil of gladness instead of mourning, and a garment of praise instead of a spirit of despair. They will be called oaks of righteousness, a planting of the LORD for the display of his splendor.

—Isa. 61:3

I Belong

Lonely, empty, lying there,
Staring into open air.
Breeze gently blowing through my hair,
My heart longing to share.

God hears my cry and settles down
Right beside me on the ground,
Drawing close, His arms surround.
Tender love abounds.

He whispers sweetness in my ears,
Calming all my childhood fears,
Collecting from my eyes the tears
That have been locked away for years.

Feeling God right next to me,
My loneliness begins to flee.
My life in Him has set me free,
Because I belong to Him, you see.

He gives me strength to carry on,
Builds me up till doubt is gone.
Through darkest nights He brings the dawn.
And turns this duckling into a swan.

Nehemiah said, "Go and enjoy choice food and sweet drinks, and send some to those who have nothing prepared. This day is sacred to our Lord. Do not grieve, for the joy of the LORD is your strength."

—Neh. 8:10

Joy of the Lord

God is in control . . .
Don't you know?
We're held in the palm of His hand.
There is never a day
That He won't show
The way for His children to stand.
He's authored our faith
He gave His decrees
Though we may not always understand.
God will work it out
Of this we are sure
When we live our lives by His command.
Let us not grow weary;
He'll finish His work
As we take hold of all God has planned.
Joy is a gift
Deeply rooted in faith
When we're fixed on the Promised Land.
For the joy of the Lord
Is the strength in our lives
And a commitment of faith it demands.

Because he has set his love upon Me, therefore will I deliver him.

—Ps. 91:14a (NKJV)

Deliverance

Deliver me, Lord, from my enemies.
Pluck me from this stormy sea.
Set me high upon a rock.
Set this captive free.

That evil knows You're in control
Makes our troubles small and our faith grow.
We surrender our hearts to You, oh Lord,
Letting Your glory show.

Then Hannah prayed and said: "My heart rejoices in the LORD; in the LORD my horn is lifted high. My mouth boasts over my enemies, for I delight in your deliverance."

—1 Sam. 2:1

Because I Prayed

Just so you know, in the matter of a day
I've come full circle because I prayed
That God would help me find my way,
Disarming the anger I kept at bay.

It's the uncommon person who can let go
Of the pain and hurt that others show.
But God will help forgiveness flow,
And through us the light of Christ will glow.

Because I prayed, God reached out and placed His hand in mine.
He led me through the raging storm, till it calmed and all was fine.
By His power and by His might, He helps me walk the line.
Each day as I come closer to His table where I'll dine.

Then I thanked my loving God and praised Him for His care.
He has become my Rock and Refuge, all because of prayer.
And when I'm feeling alone and lost, I become more aware
That He's always watching over me and when I call Him, He
   is there.

O LORD, you have searched me and you know me. You know when I sit and when I rise; you perceive my thoughts from afar. You discern my going out and my lying down; you are familiar with all my ways. Before a word is on my tongue you know it completely, O LORD.

—Ps. 139:1-4

Divine Connection

My heart is ever grateful
To the Lord for answered prayer.
When I send up my requests to Him,
I know He's always there.

He listens with His faithful ears
To every word I say.
He does what's best to grant for me
The things I ask and pray.

Sometimes He doesn't answer
In the way I think He should.
But through the years I've trusted Him
For all He does is good.

When I sit and listen
In the silence of the night,
I sometimes hear Him whisper,
"Child, it will be all right."

Divine Connection

There's nothing I can't tell Him,
For He already knows.
But every time I open up,
The bond between us grows.

I'm glad for this connection
Between my God and me,
For never will I be alone
Because I know the God Who sees.

And so we know and rely on the love God has for us. God is love. Whoever lives in love lives in God and God in him.

—1 John 4:16

God's Love

God is love.
Love is God.
They are one and the same.

We love Him
Because He first loved us.
He's called us all by name.

Nothing that we do
Will matter in the least,
Without love present in the midst.

All will pass away,
Ceasing to exist,
But love remains the everlasting gift.

How do we love like this?
God's given us His grace,
Kindness and favor undeserved.

Because of God's great love,
Christ came and took our sin.
By faith, a place with Him has been reserved.

God's Love

Let's count it as great joy
To serve others by His grace,
Bringing praise and glory to His name.

For it is by God's grace that we are saved
And by faith that we receive
His power to attain our eternal aim.

He lifted me out of the slimy pit, out of the mud and mire; he set my feet on a rock and gave me a firm place to stand.
—Ps. 40:2

Faithful, Loving Father

When life looks hopeless, I won't despair,
For God my Father's waiting there
To lift me up when I've fallen down
And can't pick myself up off the ground.

As He sits me up in that deep dark place,
He shines His light upon my face
And reassures that He's right there,
Attending to my every care.

God gives His strength so I can climb
Out of the pit, all in His time.
Along the way He shows me things
To dispel the sadness evil brings.

God is my hope to stay the course.
Unchanging, steady, my life's force.
His faithful love will spur me on,
Till the dark of night is finally gone.

Thank You, God, for Who You are,
A loving Father, never far;
A willing friend to share the load
And walk with me along life's road.

Faithful, Loving Father

I praise You, Father, Savior, Lord
For the healing power of Your Word;
For eternal life through Your only Son,
And that through Him, life's battles are won.

Set up road signs; put up guideposts. Take note of the highway, the road that you take.

—Jer. 31:21a

Marking the Trail

Going in circles,
Chasing my tail
Just sets me on
A path to fail.

Exhausted and dizzy,
I stop and pray
For God to show me
His perfect way.

I mark the trail
That took me round
With a big red X
To avoid that ground.

I place an arrow
Pointing home,
Trusting to follow
The way God has shown.

"Am I only a God nearby," declares the Lord, *"and not a God far away? Can anyone hide in secret places so that I cannot see him?"* declares the Lord. *"Do not I fill heaven and earth?"* declares the Lord.

—Jer. 23:23-24

Why Do I Run from You, Lord?

Why, Lord, do I run from You,
Resisting Your embrace?
What's this fear inside of me
That makes me hide my face?
Could it be shame for all I've done
Throwing me off course?
Would it be the guilt of secrecy
That is the driving force?
When will I stop running?
When will I finally see
That there is nowhere I can hide
That Your eyes are not on me?
Lord, help me stand before you.
Help me to understand
The depth of what my Jesus did
While human in this land.
"He took your sins upon Him
By His blood you've been made clean.
There is no need to run, child.
He loves you more than anything."
Thank You, God, my Father,
For giving me Your Son
To wash the filth of sin away
Till my time on earth is done.

May God himself, the God of peace, sanctify you through and through. May your whole spirit, soul and body be kept blameless at the coming of our Lord Jesus Christ. The one who calls you is faithful and he will do it.

—1 Thess. 5:23-24

When I Fall

Relying on myself,
I've made a mess of things.
Tried to make it right,
Could not escape shame's sting.

I couldn't face You, Lord.
I put You in a box.
Closed the lid up tight,
Making sure it locks.

I hid the box away
So that I wouldn't see
Your disappointed eyes
Looking down at me.

Little did I know
You couldn't be contained.
Reaching Your hand towards me,
You gently called my name.

"My child, it's okay.
You don't have to fret.
Come on back to Me.
I'm not finished with you yet."

"In this way they will lay up treasure for themselves as a firm foundation for the coming age, so that they may take hold of the life that is truly life."

—1 Tim. 6:19

Empty Canvas

Pink streaks through the sky,
Sun is on the rise,
Another day is dawning right before your eyes.

Like an empty canvas waiting to be painted,
Clean and white and new,
Starting fresh, untainted.

Where will you begin, what colors will you choose
To make the masterpiece
That's waiting for you?

The tools you've been given are set forth in God's Word.
A palette full of promises
Of things you've read and heard.

Take hold of the paintbrush, don't hesitate to start.
Ask God for direction
Give Him reign over your heart.

The strokes upon the canvas surely will reflect,
His light that is within you
Helping the brush connect.

Hand in Hand with God

Letting God work through you from beginning to day's end;
The masterpiece created
Will be just what God intends.

The canvas is all full now, step back and take a look.
All day you were God's paintbrush
Just see the care He took.

Unique in every aspect, painted with great care.
His strokes of love surround you
Filling up that canvas bare.

Breathtaking is the only way it can be described,
The picture that's before you
And all it holds inside.

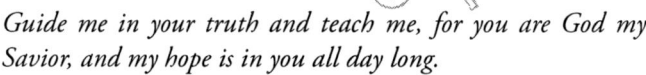

Guide me in your truth and teach me, for you are God my Savior, and my hope is in you all day long.
—Ps. 25:5

God's Truth

One step forward, two steps back,
That's the way life goes.
Don't let it throw you out of whack,
Hold on to what you know.

For God's truth never changes,
And our response to it should grow;
As we come to learn it better,
Our reactions won't be so slow.

So find out what He has to say,
In His Word you'll catch the flow.
Then carry it deep within your heart,
And pull it out when you're feeling low.

Therefore do not worry about tomorrow, for tomorrow will worry about itself. Each day has enough trouble of its own.
—Matt. 6:34

Worry

Worry robs our joy,
Wastes a lot of time,
Gives way to undue stress,
Keeps us from feeling fine.

It's out of our control.
There's nothing we can do.
Thoughts are racing in our heads.
Problems start to stew.

Anxiety and fear
Begin to build inside.
Doom is all we hear
When trusting God subsides.

Peace cannot be found
If we focus on ourselves.
We must firmly stand our ground
And take God off the shelf.

Open the container
That we've carefully placed Him in.
He is our Sustainer
Freeing us from worry's sin.

Worry

In Him we need not wonder
Or ever be afraid.
If life seems to pull us under
There are provisions that He's made.

Accept the gift of grace
He's bestowed upon our days.
All He asks is faith.
Trust in all His ways.

God's promises hold true.
Put them to the test
Release your point of view
And God will do the rest.

He will lift us up
Give us strength to quell the storm.
He'll help us drink our cup
And keep us from feeling worn.

So let's surrender all our cares
Into God's loving arms.
Our burdens He will gladly bear,
Protecting us from harm.

I have seen something else under the sun: The race is not to the swift or the battle to the strong, nor does food come to the wise or wealth to the brilliant or favor to the learned; but time and chance happen to them all.

—Eccl. 9:11

Slow Down

Rushing traffic, flashing lights,
Crowded sidewalks, what a sight!
People, people everywhere,
Hurrying, scurrying here and there.

Busy, busy all the day
Never time to stop and pray.
We rarely greet our fellow man,
For that may interrupt our plan.

What is it that we're living for?
We fill our days, but there must be more.
As I stand and watch this harried scene,
People all together, yet alone it seems.

Each person on his shoulders bears
His own burden, his own care.
If only we could switch our gears
From high to low, allowing God to steer.

Then our relationships would surely grow,
As we let life run with the Spirit's flow.
Our focus then would be on God,
Blocking off the road that Satan trods.

Slow Down

For he's the one roaming back and forth,
Making busyness seem the source of worth.
Yet if we take the time to see,
Our life in Christ is value's key.

So let's slow down and cherish time.
Wasting it would be a crime.
God gives life and takes away.
Make time for Jesus every day.

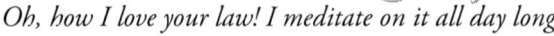

Oh, how I love your law! I meditate on it all day long.
—Ps. 119:97

Cast all your anxiety on him because he cares for you.
—1 Peter 5:7

Keep Him in the Center of Your Day

When dark clouds come your way
Get on your knees and pray.
Praise the Lord for everything you have.

If worry steals your joy
With all your strength employ
Your will to choose to give it all to Him.

When anxious thoughts creep in
Giving way to doubt and sin,
Cry out to God to make His presence known.

For it will always be your choice
To trust Him and rejoice
In the promise of the peace He will bestow.

With gentleness and grace
God gives you the space
To decide in which direction you will go.

So resist the devil's charms
And run into God's arms.
He's just waiting for the day that you will come.

Keep Him in the Center of Your Day

When the two of you embrace
And you look into His face
All your fears will simply melt away.

His love will fill your heart
Never to depart
When you keep Him in the center of your day.

If we live, we live to the Lord; and if we die, we die to the Lord. So, whether we live or die, we belong to the Lord.

—Rom. 14:8

Living for the Lord

Many times things get in the way
Of offering myself to You each day.

Lord, I want to yield my will to You,
To give my best in everything I do.

Surrendering my life into Your hands,
Placing You before the world's demands.

Take me, Lord; mold me as You wish
To do the work You want me to accomplish.

May living for You be my highest goal,
Giving up my life to Your control.

Guide me in the way that I shall go.
Use me, Lord, so all the world will know

That You are God, Lord of all the earth.
Your sacrifice has brought us new birth.

Holy Spirit, fill me with Your fire,
Seeking what it is that You desire.

Living for the Lord

Living for You is my greatest treasure,
Encouraged by a love beyond all measure.

In You death is life and life is death.
I'm here to serve You till my final breath.

May I make my days count for You alone,
For Your glory, Your kingdom, and Your throne.

Your mercy and Your grace have brought me to this place.
I can't wait until I meet You face to face.

Lord, humbly I kneel before You now.
In thanks, let my heart express this vow

To live for You each day, letting nothing block the way,
That every moment of my life be Yours, I pray.

> *But may the righteous be glad and rejoice before God; may they be happy and joyful.*
>
> —Ps. 68:3

Lord, I Just Want to be Happy

Lord, I just want to be happy.
I want to learn to walk in Your ways,
To see the world with Your eyes.
Change my heart from complaining to praise.

Lord, I just want to be happy
I want my heart to be set on You,
Loving others sincerely
The way You want me to.

Lord, I just want to be happy
To embrace the pain in my life.
I want to know how to transform it,
Gleaning something joyful from my strife.

Lord, I just want to be happy.
I am aware this life is rough.
Even in the midst of suffering,
I want You to be enough.

Lord, I just want to be happy.
I want to grab hold of Your grace,
Live my life contently
No matter what circumstance I face.

Lord, I Just Want to be Happy

Lord, I just want to be happy.
I want to seek You in the storm,
Anchor myself to You
When life's problems start to swarm.

Lord, I just want to be happy.
You have made me to this end
To experience joy, love, and peace
When on You I depend.

Lord, You have made me happy.
Now that I'm rooted in Your love,
You've given me the tools I need
To take my trials and rise above.

What does it mean to be happy?
Look to God and you will see
That He is the only answer
In our search to be happy.

But store up for yourselves treasures in heaven, where moth and rust do not destroy, and where thieves do not break in and steal.
—Matt. 6:20

All for You Today

Lord, help us leave the past behind
And focus on You today.
No worries of the future,
Just trusting day by day.
Everything we do,
Everything we say,
May it all be for Your glory
As heavenly treasures we lay.

For I am convinced that neither death nor life, neither angels nor demons, neither the present nor the future, nor any powers, neither height nor depth, nor anything else in all creation, will be able to separate us from the love of God that is in Christ Jesus our Lord.
—Rom. 8:38-39

Morning Routine

Each morning I wake,
Sit up in my bed,
Stretch out my arms,
And scratch my head.

Thanking the Lord,
Praising Him as I pray
For the breath of life
He's put in me today.

I hop out of bed,
My feet hit the floor.
I throw on my armor,
And head for the door.

I've got on my helmet,
My shield, and my sword.
Belt buckled, feet ready
With the truth of God's Word.

Hand in Hand with God

Now I'm prepared
For those fiery darts
Aimed in the direction
Of my heart.

There's nothing to fear
With God on my side.
There's no separation
Where His love abides.

Finally, be strong in the Lord and in his mighty power. Put on the full armor of God so that you can take your stand against the devil's schemes.

—Eph. 6:10-11

God's Armor

Put on the whole armor of God
That we may withstand in the evil day
When we've done all we can to stand
Wearing the armor of protection, begin to pray.

Lord, I'm buckling Your belt of truth
Around my waist today.
Please send the truth of Your Word
To blast Satan's lies away.

This day I don the breastplate
Of Your holy righteousness.
I'll shed the garments of my shame.
Through You my life is blessed.

I'm putting on the shoes
Of readiness and peace.
Help me to stand firmly.
Help my confidence increase.

Lord, today I'm picking up
Your perfect shield of faith
To deflect the fiery arrows
That Satan shoots my way.

Hand in Hand with God

The helmet of salvation
Will fit right upon my head.
You redeemed me at a high cost
When You died for me instead.

Lord, let me wield the Spirit's sword,
Armed with Your holy Word,
Using scripture as the weapon
To stand against the lies I've heard.

Thank You for Your armor, Lord,
And the promise of protection,
Equipping me with all I need
To stand firm in Your reflection.

And the peace of God, which transcends all understanding, will guard your hearts and your minds in Christ Jesus.
—Phil. 4:7

Thinking Differently

What are the things that you're telling yourself?
Are your thoughts causing you distress?
Do you constantly put yourself down if you fail?
Are you quick to second guess?

How do you measure your successes?
How do you view yourself?
Is it through the eyes of God as He sees you?
Or through the eyes of someone else?

Do you want to be free of this thinking?
To look at yourself differently?
I will let you in on a secret . . .
You must understand how our God sees.

You are His creation.
He calls you by name.
Masterfully, He forms every detail.
You were made to bring Him fame.

The possibilities are endless
If following God is your choice.
You'll be set apart as holy
As you listen to His voice.

Hand in Hand with God

Train your mind to think upon good things,
That which is lovely, pure, and true.
Doing this will secure the promise
That God's peace will come shining through.

Finally brothers, whatever is true, what ever is noble, what ever is right, whatever is pure, whatever is lovely, whatever is admirable . . . if anything is excellent or praiseworthy . . . think about such things.

—Phil. 4:8

What Do You Think?

Let us set our thoughts on what's noble and true,
Lovely and pure and admirable too.

Things that are pure, praiseworthy, and right,
On these things we shall set our sights.

Reject those thoughts that bring us down,
Preventing Satan from coming round.

Then the peace of God will reign supreme,
And our hearts and minds He will redeem.

And call upon me in the day of trouble; I will deliver you, and you will honor me.

—Ps. 50:15

Our Days

Our days are filled with ups and downs,
Smiles and frowns,
Joys and sorrows,
Hopes for tomorrow.

Our days are filled with give and take,
Success and mistakes,
Life and death,
Till our final breath.

Our days are filled with found and lost,
Gain and cost,
Win and lose.
What will we choose?

Our days are filled with opposites,
Misses and hits,
Yeses and noes.
That's how life goes.

How will we go about our days?
Follow Jesus in His ways
By reacting well
So the world can tell . . .

Our Days

That Jesus is Lord of our life,
In good times or in strife,
Peace time or at war.
In Him we will weather the storm.

Do not take revenge, my friends, but leave room for God's wrath, for it is written: "It is mine to avenge; I will repay," says the Lord. On the contrary: "If your enemy is hungry, feed him; if he is thirsty, give him something to drink. In doing this, you will heap burning coals on his head." Do not be overcome by evil, but overcome evil with good.

—Rom. 12:19-21

The Opposite Practice

Sing praise to the Lord when you're feeling blue,
Though it goes against what you want to do.
Thank Him for all the battles He's won
And the hurdles you've already overcome.

Try not to dwell on the problem at hand
But on learning to live by God's command.
Hiding His Word deep down in your heart
Will give you the perfect place to start.

Don't let your feelings define who you are,
For you are God's child and He'll search wide and far
To bring you into His loving arms
Where He'll shepherd and shelter and keep you from harm.

So let's practice the principle of opposites.
When down, practice up to stay out of life's pits.
In fear display courage; when angry, you bless;
And when you are sad, proclaim happiness.

The Opposite Practice

Becoming aware that you feel as you do,
Instead of the feeling becoming you,
Is an insightful key to emotional health
And a skill we must master, then share the wealth!

May the God of hope fill you with all joy and peace as you trust in him, so that you may overflow with hope by the power of the Holy Spirit.

—Rom. 15:13

Can You Still Use Me Broken?

Oh, Holy Spirit,
Where do you go?
Some days you're with me,
Some I don't know.

When I'm feeling happy,
You fill me up.
But in days of great sorrow,
You drain from my cup.

With each bout of sadness,
Another crack forms.
My cup is all broken
From numerous storms.

Can You still use me broken?
Do You mind that I leak?
You'll have to fill me more often
To make me strong when I'm weak.

Am I worth the trouble?
Those cracks are quite large.
It'll take lots of effort,

Can You Still Use Me Broken?

But I'll leave You in charge.

Oh, Holy Spirit,
I know where You go.
You are always with me
And around me You flow.

Thank You, dear Jesus,
For leaving Your Spirit here
To be my Helper
Who comforts my fears.

Yet, O LORD, you are our Father. We are the clay, you are the potter; we are all the work of your hand.

—Isa. 64:8

If I Could Be . . .

If I could be a bird
And fly far, far away,
High above the chaotic world.
I would surely not delay.
Soaring swiftly through the air
With nothing in the way,
Not a care or worry
To clutter up my day.

If I could be a butterfly
Emerging from a cocoon,
In all my stunning beauty,
I'd surely take off soon.
Fluttering above the earth,
Whistling a tune,
Floating on the currents,
Free as a lost balloon.

If I could be a flower
Bursting from the ground,
Growing tall in stature
With petals all around,
Then I'd be admired
Wherever I was found
For my fragrant aroma
And vibrant colors that abound.

If I Could Be . . .

If I could be a gentle rain
Falling from the sky,
Watering the earth below,
Quenching its thirsty cry,
Bringing new life to the landscape.
As I water all that's dry,
Then I'd hear creation sing
Every time I would come by.

There are just so many things
That I would like to be;
The sun, the moon, a twinkling star,
A wave born in the sea.
And yet, I think I'll be content
Just knowing that I'm free,
For God has made me special,
So I think I'll just be me.

I have told you these things, so that in me you may have peace. In this world you will have trouble. But take heart! I have overcome the world.

—John 16:33

Trouble in this Life

Troubles present themselves every day in this life of mine.
Please, Lord, help me handle them with wisdom.
Sometimes they get the best of me
And my reactions aren't so kind.
Grant me patience, Lord, that I may make it through them.

Is it any wonder that there's suffering in this life
When as Christians our foundation is the cross?
It shouldn't come as much surprise
When trouble and chaos strike.
It's our opportunity to hold on to our Boss!

These things come up to show the world
Just where our true faith lies.
In the One Whose love is really all we need.
The words and lies of Satan are always being hurled,
Deceiving us that God won't hear our cries.

But God gives us this promise, He will help us stand.
He's an ever present help in times of trouble.
When in Him we place our trust,
Our Lord takes us by the hand,
He offers grace and He delights to give us double.

Trouble in this Life

We thank You, dear Lord Jesus, for giving us Your all.
The cost was great in the sacrifice You made.
Through You we have inheritance
When we accept Your call.
May our undying praise and gratitude not fade.

In the same way, let your light shine before men, that they may see your good deeds and praise your Father in heaven.
—Matt. 5:16

Jesus in Me

As I go through trials, what do others see?
Can they see Jesus living inside of me?

How do I handle my stresses each day?
Do the pressures of life cause me to stray?

Am I standing firm on the things I profess?
And when I mess up, am I quick to confess?

Do I trust in God for my needs and provision?
Or do I worry and fret over every decision?

Are my thoughts of all things pure, lovely, and good?
Am I guarding my heart as God says I should?

Do I take enough time with Jesus each day?
To talk with Him, walk with Him, and just sit and pray?

Am I patient and kind with the people I meet?
Do I smile and acknowledge those I pass in the street?

Living for Jesus is my greatest goal.
Becoming just like Him in heart, mind, and soul.

I want to make sure that people can see
That it's not by my own power, but Jesus in me.

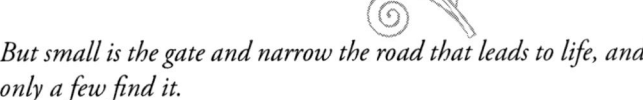

But small is the gate and narrow the road that leads to life, and only a few find it.

—Matt. 7:14

Walking in His Way

In the silence of the morning, I sit and think of You.
The day ahead unfolds before my eyes.
I give to You the plans I have, set firmly in my mind
To bless and help me to prioritize.

Since I've come to know You, Lord, I look forward to this time,
Of Your instruction in the way I should proceed.
Your walking right beside me through every move I make
Gives me confidence that my plans will succeed.

I will put my trust in You, Lord, take me by the hand,
In faith I will follow what You say.
Instill in me the courage to walk the narrow path
So I won't slip into the worldly way.

Not too many understand the faith I place in You
Believing in someone I cannot see.
But in holding on to You, dear Lord, I will not be shaken.
Help me live so that You shine brightly through me.

Now if we are children, then we are heirs-heirs of God and co-heirs with Christ, if indeed we share in his sufferings in order that we may also share in His glory.

—Rom. 8:17

The Inheritance

I am Your child.
My love for You grows
With each waking moment
Its evidence shows.

The peace that You've promised
I chose to receive
Encompassed my heart,
Because I believe.

Beyond all understanding
Your mercies bestowed.
And though I'm not worthy,
Abounding grace flowed.

As a powerful force
You cut through like a knife
Changing forever
My pitiful life.

Reborn of Your Spirit
Old became new.
Now my whole focus
Is forever on You!

The Inheritance

I desire to serve You,
To seek Your sweet face,
To live my life for You,
Accepting Your grace.

With love in Your eyes
Upon me You gaze.
I bow down before You
In worship and praise.

Thank You for saving
My life from despair.
An inheritance waits,
Because I am Your heir.

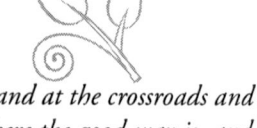

This is what the LORD says: "Stand at the crossroads and look; ask for the ancient paths, ask where the good way is, and walk in it, and you will find rest for your souls."

—Jer. 6:16

The Journey

We are all on a pilgrimage through this life.
Aliens in a foreign land.
Faced with both joy and strife,
Bound by created time, led by God's own hand.

Each day we're alive is a journey of faith.
Placed *in* this world but not *of* it.
We shall not store up our treasure in this place,
But in our eternal lives through the Spirit.

All who believe have a special plan,
Laid out even before we were born.
God equipped us for travel as only He can.
Giving strength, that we not become worn.

Successfully navigating the time that we're here
Depends greatly on our trusting Him.
Many times we are tempted to give in to fear
When we fail to let God in.

Brothers and sisters, walk together in love,
Spurring each other on,
Keeping our eyes towards our homeland above,
Walking the same road those before us have gone.

The Journey

When one of us finally makes it to the end of the road,
In heaven and earth there is great celebration.
God welcomes them to His glorious abode,
And all the faithful sing with triumphant jubilation!

Let's view our time on earth with the expectant joy
Of knowing God's waiting for us to arrive.
Cheering us on as His gifts we employ
To accomplish His plan, to become fully alive.

Throughout our journey we will see through a glass that is dim,
But as we grow closer to the place He's prepared
And our eyes are set firmly in glory on Him,
We will see with new eyes through a glass that is clear.

We can only imagine the splendor we'll see
As we reach our destination.
God's pure love will set us free,
Then we'll experience full restoration.

It's this promise and hope that will see us through,
Keeping this in mind helps us stand.
Giving glory to God for all that we do
Till we get to the Promised Land!

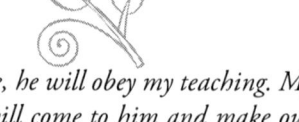

Jesus replied, "If anyone loves me, he will obey my teaching. My Father will love him, and we will come to him and make our home with him."

—John 14:23

Home Sweet Home

I made a little home for Him
Deep within my heart.
There wasn't much to work with,
'Cause it was broken all apart.

But from the day He entered in
That meager little home,
Transformed from a ramshackle hut,
To a castle made of precious stone.

He cleared out all the garbage,
Swept the floors all clean,
Removed every cobweb,
Making His new home just gleam!

With all these renovations
Taking place inside,
Something began to happen
To the place He now abides.

The inner beauty He created
Grew from the inside out.
His unmistakable workmanship
Became due cause to shout!

Home Sweet Home

If Jesus can make even me
Into a castle grand,
Then surely you should let Him in
To be made over by His hand!

But our citizenship is in heaven. And we eagerly await a Savior from there, the Lord Jesus Christ.

—Phil. 3:20

Heaven Bound

No greater love can there ever be,
Than the love that Jesus has for me.
He gave His life so I'd be free
From the grip of sin and the enemy.

God fashioned this world by His own hand,
And made us part of His master plan,
Equipped us with the strength to stand
On His firm foundation, not on sand.

Each of us must play his part,
In fulfilling God's plan from the start.
Lord, guard the contents of our hearts
As we raise Your shield against Satan's darts.

God's greatest gift shall not be in vain.
He gave all, so that we can gain
Eternal life. He erased our stain
When the perfect Lamb, His Son, was slain.

Jesus came to pave the way.
God opened His kingdom gates that day.
Now what we need to do is pray,
Inviting Him into our hearts to stay.

Heaven Bound

Oh, how we long to know Him more
As we stand and knock on heaven's door.
Our hearts are touched to the very core,
Anticipating what's in store.

Thank You, Lord, for Your saving grace,
That one day we might see Your face.
As we enter the gates of that great place.
We're heaven bound when we win life's race.

After this I looked and there before me was a great multitude that no one could count, from every nation, tribe, people and language, standing before the throne and in front of the Lamb. They were wearing white robes and were holding palm branches in their hands. And they cried out in a loud voice: "Salvation belongs to our God, who sits on the throne, and to the Lamb." All the angels were standing around the throne and around the elders and the four living creatures. They fell down on their faces before the throne and worshiped God, saying: "Amen! Praise and glory and wisdom and thanks and honor and power and strength be to our God for ever and ever. Amen!"

Then one of the elders asked me, "These in white robes—who are they, and where did they come from?" I answered, "Sir, you know." And he said, "These are they who have come out of the great tribulation; they have washed their robes and made them white in the blood of the Lamb. Therefore, they are before the throne of God and serve him day and night in his temple; and he who sits on the throne will spread his tent over them. Never again will they hunger; never again will they thirst. The sun will not beat upon them, nor any scorching heat. For the Lamb at the center of the throne will be their shepherd; he will lead them to springs of living water. And God will wipe away every tear from their eyes."

—Rev. 7:9-17

Heaven

Wow! Can you imagine?
When we enter heaven's gates,
The splendor set before us,
On that God-appointed date?
The table will be waiting,
As God pulls out our seat.
Dining with our Father

Heaven

In His house, oh, what a treat!
All His glory He'll reveal to us.
The grandeur of love
Will no longer be a mystery,
For we'll be with Him above.
There will be no more trouble.
All bad things will pass away.
Our hearts will be made pure as gold
When we enter on that day.
All we are will be made known.
Our minds will be transformed.
Our bodies will be made perfect,
And our will to His conformed.
There will be no more fighting,
For in heaven peace will reign.
There will be no more sinful thoughts,
For the mind of Christ we'll gain.
The sweet songs of the angels
Will permeate our souls,
Causing us to sing along
With words of praise to God extolled.
There will be no more rushing.
No longer bound by time or space,
We will revel in His majesty
When we meet Him face to face.
Suffering will be no more;
Instead, joy will abound.
Harmonious shouts and laughter
Will be heard from all around.
God will call us all together,
As His children we will come;
In the splendor of His presence,
He'll give the keys to His kingdom.
The inheritance we've hoped for

Hand in Hand with God

From the day we first believed,
Will be granted to each one of us;
As His heirs, we will receive.
All God's truth and goodness
Will be unveiled for us to see,
And love will be the means by which
We live and move and be.
Thank You, God, our Father,
For preparing us this place,
And giving us our sonship,
And supplying us Your grace.

Now we see but a poor reflection as in a mirror; then we shall see face to face. Now I know in part; then I shall know fully, even as I am fully known. And now these three remain: faith, hope and love. But the greatest of these is love.
—1 Cor. 13:12-13

Life Reflections

Looking in life's mirror
We get a clouded view.
The reflection is distorted,
Images askew.

One day we will see clearly,
Knowing all that's true.
We will come to see Him face to face,
When it's Him that we pursue.

Until that time God's left us
With these three things to do . . .
Practice faith, hope, and love
Till His work in us is through.

Do not conform any longer to the pattern of this world, but be transformed by the renewing of your mind. Then you will be able to test and approve what God's will is—his good, pleasing and perfect will.

—Rom. 12:2

The Junk Drawer

Life can be messy,
Like a packed junk drawer.
Sorting it out can be quite a chore.

My brain is a place
Where I store lots of stuff.
Thoughts in abundance, more than enough.

Ridding myself
Of the things I don't need,
Is sometimes painful indeed.

One by one
I pull each thing out.
Keeping or throwing it comes with doubt.

Its contents
Lie there for such a long time,
Becoming ingrained in my mind.

The Junk Drawer

All kinds of things
Good mixed with bad,
The most perplexing job I've ever had.

When it's finally done
It's a pleasure to see
The grand transformation in me.

> *"Now may the Lord of peace himself give you peace at all times and in every way. The Lord be with all of you."*
>
> —2 Thes. 3:16

Send Your Peace

When all the world seems frenzied,
I cry out for release.
Calm my frazzled mind, Lord,
Send to me Your peace.

My energy's depleted,
Trying to keep up
With all the things that people need.
Lord, please fill me up.

Free me from the bondage
Of the busyness of life.
Quiet down the chaos
Creating all this strife.

I'm fashioned by Your hand, Lord,
To be a human being.
I've become a human doing,
Please help me in the seeing.

Teach me to be still, Lord,
That I may learn to rest,
In the shelter of Your presence
When I am feeling stressed.

But be sure to fear the Lord and serve him faithfully with all your heart; consider what great things he has done for you.
—1 Sam. 12:24

Questions, Lord?

Lord, how can I ever thank You enough
For bringing me through all the rotten stuff?

How can You love me after the bad things I've done,
Yet over and over, You forgive each one?

Is there anything, Lord, that I can do
To show my undying thanks for You?

Is there any way that I can pay You back
For shining your light where all was black?

When will I learn that You're always there,
Watching over me with Your loving care?

Lord, why do I doubt You when life gets hard,
When You faithfully heal the parts of me that are scarred?

These questions I ask, though the answer is clear;
I'm Your child, You love me, and You count me as dear.

The only way I can ever repay
Is to live my life for You, Lord, each day.

Jesus answered, "Everyone who drinks this water will be thirsty again, but whoever drinks the water I give him will never thirst. Indeed, the water I give him will become in him a spring of water welling up to eternal life."

—John 4:13-14

The Woman at the Well

The woman at the well
Was a Samaritan.
She came to draw some water
After the others long had been.

She knew she wasn't welcome
All alone in her shame.
Her life thus far was one big mess,
But on this day that would change.

A man was sitting by the well;
He looked to be a Jew.
He asked her for a drink of water,
And now she was confused.

Jews didn't like Samaritans,
And men didn't talk to women.
What did this man want from her?
So she asked the man this question:

"How is it, Sir, that you, a Jew,
Could ask me for a drink?"
He replied, "If you knew the gift of God
You would be asking Me, I think!

The Woman at the Well

"For I supply a living water
For anyone who asks."
"But, Sir, the well is very deep.
How will you draw without a flask?"

"The water from this well
Will make you thirst again,
But the water I will give you
Springs forth God's eternal plan."

He spoke to her so gently
Like music to her ears.
"Drink my 'living water,'
Leave behind you all your fears."

At first she didn't understand
For she had been used all her life.
So she had to keep her guard up
To avoid possible strife.

"The water from this well
Will never quench your thirst.
What you need is love, my child,
That's what I'll give you first.

"Accept this gift I offer
Drink this cup and start anew."
The woman nodded, "Yes, Sir."
Then He told her what to do.

"Go call upon your husband
And then come back to me."
She said, "I have no husband."
He nodded. "You've had five, I see."

Hand in Hand with God

Her eyes got big, how did He know?
A prophet He must be.
She spoke of the Messiah's coming,
"I who speak to you am He."

She got so excited,
This really blew her mind.
She ran to tell the others,
Leaving her water jar behind.

Can you imagine meeting Jesus?
What would your reaction be?
Would you drink the living water
That He offers you and me?

At first the woman didn't recognize
Whom she was talking to.
Her focus was on other things,
Blocking Jesus from her view.

We too must be careful,
It's just the same for us today.
When we take our eyes off Jesus,
We are quickly led astray.

So let's capture the excitement
As did the woman at the well,
And leave all hindrances behind,
Grab Jesus' good news, go and tell.

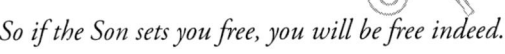

So if the Son sets you free, you will be free indeed.

—John 8:36

Jesus Came

Jesus came so that we might live
Life more abundantly.
He broke the chains that kept us bound,
Died and rose to set us free.

No greater love has there ever been
Than the sacrifice He made.
By going to the cross for us
To assure sin's debts were paid.

The grace that God bestowed on us
Is nothing we deserved.
He gave to us unselfishly
So our faith would be preserved.

Jesus paved the way for us
Right to His Father's heart.
Invited us to follow Him
Belief in Him is where we start.

Each one has a cross to bear,
We must take it up and go.
Die to self and live for Him,
So through us God's love will flow.

Hand in Hand with God

He sent His Holy Spirit
To help us on our way.
Empowered us with many gifts
If we will trust Him and obey.

It is by grace that we are saved.
He calls us each by name,
To be heirs to His heavenly throne.
This is why Jesus came.

Thank You, dear Lord Jesus
For saving us from death.
May our lives reflect Your glory
Until we take our final breath.

As the Father has loved me, so have I loved you. Now remain in my love.

—John 15:9

Matchless Love

Of all the things I've ever known
The greatest has to be
The matchless love of Jesus,
And how He came to set us free.

He walked among us on this earth
His Father's mission to complete.
Gathering people to Himself
As a shepherd herds his sheep.

He revealed to us how to teach and heal.
He showed us how to love.
He offered us new life through Him
With His Father in heaven above.

An example of the greatest faith
In God's eternal plan,
He made His way to Calvary
To take on the sin of man.

He granted us forgiveness
As He hung upon that cross,
A sacrifice to save us
From being forever lost.

Hand in Hand with God

I cannot even fathom
How He must have felt before He died.
All the ugliness of man
Heaped on Him from every side.

The filth and dirt of every sin
Mixed with His precious blood and sweat
Made Him too hideous to look at.
Darkness fell as He paid our debt.

When it was done, He cried out,
Surrendering His Spirit.
He gave everything He had for us
Redeemed us by His merit.

How can we still reject Him
After knowing what He's done?
Come to Him, give Him your life, give thanks! The battle's won!

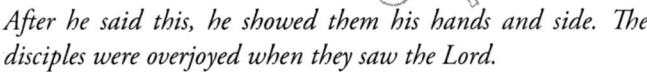

After he said this, he showed them his hands and side. The disciples were overjoyed when they saw the Lord.
—John 20:20

His Scars

Jesus bore His scars
Even after He rose,
So everyone would know
That it was He.

He could have resurrected
Leaving them behind,
But chose to keep
Them as a reminder for all to see.

For all they represent,
And all that He went through,
Tell the story
Of what we mean to Him.

It is by these scars we know
The sacrifice He made
And God's victory
Over death and sin.

We are to do the same
As our dear Jesus did,
Displaying our scars
To make known

Hand in Hand with God

The reason that we're healed
Is due to God's great love,
And our testimony
Helps God's seeds to be sown.

Once our wounds are healed,
Let's not hide them
From each other.
Display the scars for all the world to see.

So that everyone will know
The wonders of God's love.
That His Word is truth,
And it will set us free.

Thank You, God our Father,
Through Jesus Christ Your Son,
For revealing to us
All we need to know;

And giving us the chance
To follow Jesus' way,
Dying to the flesh
So the Spirits' work within our lives will show.

And by that will, we have been made holy through the sacrifice of the body of Jesus Christ once for all.
—Heb. 10:10

Through Jesus, therefore, let us continually offer to God a sacrifice of praise—the fruit of lips that confess his name.
—Heb. 13:15

For You and for Me

Look up at the cross, what do you see?
Can you see Jesus hanging for you and for me?

Look at the thorns that crown His head,
The pain on His face and the blood that was shed.

His side, hands, and feet were pierced by a spear.
The wounds He bore to draw us near.

The worst kind of death, He suffered for us.
Bearing our sin to bring justice.

To a broken world, full of disgrace,
He sacrificed all. He won our case.

Can you see your name written in His wounds?
His determined look to save the world from doom?

Can you even imagine the pain He endured,
Beaten and bloodied, insulted and scorned?

Hand in Hand with God

He walked that road to Calvary
And broke sin's curse for you and me.

Will you accept His gift to you;
Take hold the redemption that's made you new?

No greater love could there ever be
Than what He has done for you and for me.

Let us thank Him then, for His work on the cross
By believing and trusting and counting the cost.

Giving Him honor, and glory, and praise
As we worship Him fervently all of our days.

Take my yoke upon you and learn from me, for I am gentle and humble in heart, and you will find rest for your souls. For my yoke is easy and my burden is light.

—Matt. 11:29-30

Lay it All Down

The foot of the cross is the place to be
When life's burdens weigh too heavily.

God gave us this place to lay it all down,
Releasing our pressures on holy ground.

Instead of succumbing to life demands,
Let us be led by His command.

"Come to me all who are weary and tired.
Rest I will give when you're feeling expired.

"My yoke is easy; My burden is light.
I will guide you through the dark of night.

"Let Me cast all of your fears aside.
Sit at My feet; where you'll safely abide."

He holds us securely in the palm of His hand,
In His refuge we can firmly stand.

There is victory living our lives for Him.
When we surrender control and let Him in.

But thanks be to God! He gives us the victory through our Lord Jesus Christ.

—1 Cor. 15:57

Victory

Jesus walked the road to Calvary.
Died to set us free.
Gave all for you and me.
No greater love can be.

Sacrificed His life for all.
Victory was the call.
Saved us from the fall.
New life He did install.

His atonement for our sin
Assures us that we'll win
The battle we are in,
Because now we are His kin.

God takes care of His own,
Like none we've ever known.
The seeds of love He's sown,
Inside our hearts have grown.

Now with the overflow
Of God's love, let us show
Each other how to grow
In Christ, so all will know

Victory

That He's the One Who saves,
Worthy of our praise,
Loving Jesus all our days,
As we follow in His ways.

Thank You, mighty One,
For sending us Your Son.
So we no longer have to run,
Because You have overcome!

For God so loved the world that he gave his one and only Son, that whoever believes in him shall not perish but have eternal life.

—John 3:16

RSVP

Jesus our Redeemer,
The Bread of Life You are.
Your love's scaled every mountain
And healed up every scar.
You were pierced for our transgressions,
Paid the debt for all our sin,
All so You could loose us
From the chains of death we were in.
You gave the invitation
To all who will believe.
RSVP to God Himself,
And eternal life we will receive.

I guide you in the way of wisdom and lead you along straight paths.

—Prov. 4:11

GPS (God's Positioning System)

We may have to go through some pain,
But God will keep us sane.

We may be bombarded with insults,
But God will control the results.

We may screw up and lose it all,
But God's there to catch our fall.

We may feel weary and troubled,
But we then find God's grace has been doubled.

We may really want to give up,
But in those moments He fills our cup.

It seems no matter our circumstance,
Trusting God brings a second chance.

He'll guide us along the straight path,
Shielding us from Satan's wrath.

Acknowledging God in all we do,
Helps us hold on to what is true.

Thank You, God, for the security we find in You!

> "For I know the plans I have for you," declares the LORD, "plans to prosper you and not to harm you, plans to give you hope and a future."
>
> —Jer. 29:11

God's Plan For Me

God has a wonderful plan for me, but I don't know what it is . . .
There are so many things I want to try, but those I succeed with are few.
I guess through trial and error, I'll figure out what God wants.
I will try not to get frustrated with myself when I fail to follow through.

It doesn't mean I'm a failure, or that I'm not good enough.
God applauds me for trying, comforts me when I fall, and cheers when I get back up.
He walks behind and before me and surrounds me on either side.
When things don't work out and I'm empty, He is faithful to refill my cup.

Maybe it's God's way of saying this is not the thing for me . . .
So I let it go and try something else. I don't let discouragement get in the way.
Nothing I do will be wasted, though it may not be God's plan.
I'll keep seeking His will for the answer every time I pray.

And this is what he promised us—even eternal life.
—1 John 2:25

Eternal Perspective

Prepare to live
With this in mind . . .
Eternal perspective.
Then you will find
That problems
Seem a little less.
Small irritations
Cause less stress.
For when you know
You're just passing through,
The things you sow
Are done with that view.
And the reaping time
Will be ever so sweet,
When you choose to recline
At Jesus' feet.
Bring Him all
You're worldly cares,
So you won't fall
Into Satan's snares.
Standing firm
On His foundation,
You'll have no concern
Of your salvation.
'Cause His life He gave
For you and me,
Only He can save

Hand in Hand with God

For eternity.
Grab hold this gift,
Jesus' sacrifice.
Let your spirit lift,
As you gain new life.
Know He was sent
To erase sin's stain.
Let His atonement
Not be in vain.
Prepare to live
With this in mind . . .
Eternal perspective
Then you will find
The struggles you face
In your journey here
Will be met with grace
Instead of fear.

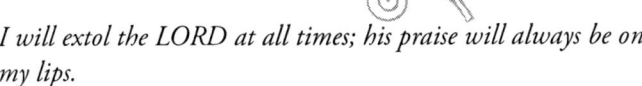

I will extol the LORD at all times; his praise will always be on my lips.

—Psalm 34:1

Praise to God

Give praise to God our Father
Who watches from above.
He hems us in, behind, before,
He showers us with love.

In Him we never are alone.
In Him there's truth and life.
Protected by His sword and shield,
He rescues us from strife.

Cry out to God our Father.
Bring glory to His name.
In everything we do and say,
Be sure to bring Him fame.

For He alone is holy.
It's Him we long to serve.
We worship and adore Him,
From His path we'll never swerve.

God's steady, faithful goodness,
We can count on all our days.
When we take hold our eternal life,
And follow in His ways.

Hand in Hand with God

Yes, for God so loved the world
That He gave His only Son.
And whoever believes and follows Him,
Eternal life's begun.

We love You, mighty, awesome God
With our hearts, minds, and souls.
Trusting in Your every word,
We press on towards the goal.

Give praise to God our Father,
He is our All in All.
Instilling in us peace and joy
When we listen to His call.

And this gospel of the kingdom will be preached in the whole world as a testimony to all nations, and then the end will come.
—Matt. 24:14

The Message

God's given a message
That He wants you to share.
It's a message of redemption,
Of love and hope and care.

From the moment you accept Him,
You're commissioned to go forth;
Bearing witness for His kingdom,
Reaching south, east, west, and north.

Telling the story
Of life-giving change,
How when Jesus entered
Your heart wasn't the same.

He opened you up
To a love you've not known.
Gave His life as a sacrifice,
The greatest love ever shown.

God took all your sins
Forgiving each one,
Put them all on the cross
With Jesus His Son.

Hand in Hand with God

You have every reason
To go out and tell
Of the wonderful mercy
You now know full well.

Grace has been showered,
Now what will you do?
Keep it all to yourself?
Or pass on the news?

Your life has been spared
From the depths of the pit.
Will you stand up and shout it,
Or on this gift will you sit?

Today is the day.
What will you choose?
There's a dynamite message,
Will you dare light the fuse?

Blowing the lid off
This world's point of view
Gives God the glory
That He alone is due.

Sing to the Lord, for he has done glorious things; let this be known to all the world.
—Isa. 12:5

Worship the Lord with gladness; come before him with joyful songs.
—Ps. 100:2

Shout Out Your Song

Shout out your song to the Lord!
Come before Him with dancing and praise!
Proclaiming His Holy Word,
Worship Him all of your days!

Carry His banner of love
To everybody you meet.
Just as a hand fills a glove
God will make your life complete.

Hide His name in your heart,
That you might not sin against Him.
Now is a great time to start!
So open up and let Him in!

Thank God for all He has done.
He's prepared a place for you.
Through the sacrifice of His Son,
He's washed you clean and made you new.

Hand in Hand with God

We love You, Lord, mighty God,
King of Kings.
Your saving grace
Makes our hearts sing!

Lift your hands to the Lord!
Sing out with songs of joy!
Give your life to Him.
Hallelujah!

Sing to him, sing praise to him; tell of all his wonderful acts.
—1 Chron. 16:9

All for You, Jesus

Worship and praise Him all of your days!
Adore Him and sing about everything!
Give thanks and rejoice by lifting your voice!
Follow His ways all of your days!
Bow down before Him, because He's conquered sin!
Honor His name by proclaiming His fame!
Surrender your life into His hands. By His strength He'll help you stand!
Glorify Him in all you do because of His great love for you!
Thank You, dear Jesus, for all that You've done; by Your work on the cross the battle's been won!
All for You, Jesus, on earth we will strive, because it's by Your sacrifice that we are alive!

I am the good shepherd; I know my sheep and my sheep know me, just as the Father knows me and I know the Father, and I lay down my life for the sheep.

—John 10:14-15

Shepherd and Sheep

The shepherd gathers his sheep in his arms.
He keeps them from going astray.
He leads them into green pastures,
Providing for them night and day.

Sheep know the voice of their shepherd.
They listen and there they will go.
Completely trusting his every word,
For his care is all that they know.

Sheep can be foolish creatures,
Stubborn and curious things.
They wander away to investigate
What the grass in the other field brings.

Sometimes the sheep find trouble,
Fall down and can't get up on their own.
The shepherd sets out to rescue them,
Giving comfort and leading them home.

Jesus is our Good Shepherd.
We are the flock in His care.
When we obediently follow,
He'll lead us to the place He's prepared.

Shepherd and Sheep

We, as sheep, can be foolish,
Trying to go our own way,
Putting ourselves in danger,
When from the flock we stray.

But Jesus, knowing our weakness
Goes and seeks out His lost.
He's made Himself the sacrifice;
Let us never forget the cost.

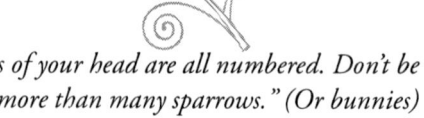

"Indeed, the very hairs of your head are all numbered. Don't be afraid; you are worth more than many sparrows." (Or bunnies) Parenthesis mine.
—Luke 12:7

Bunnies

I pulled into my driveway
And there before my eyes,
Stood three little bunnies.
I caught them by surprise.

I looked at them,
And they looked at me.
When I opened up my car door,
They darted wildly.

One ran forward.
One ran back.
The third little bunny
Was frozen in its tracks.

I tried to reassure them.
I meant to cause no harm.
"You need not run away from me."
I turned on all my charm.

From where they were, the two that ran,
Turned around to look.
Their frozen little friend stared,
As its tiny body shook.

Bunnies

"I didn't mean to scare you;
I am friend, not foe.
Please continue playing,
It's time for me to go."

So I walked up the driveway,
And as I glanced around,
I saw those bunnies hopping.
A truce that day was found.

I watched them from my window
For a couple minutes more.
Happy little bunnies,
Frolicking on earth's grassy floor.

O Lord, what a variety of things you have made! In wisdom you have made them all. The earth is full of your creatures. Here is the ocean, vast and wide, teeming with life of every kind, both large and small. See the ships sailing along, and Leviathan, which you made to play in the sea.

—Ps. 104:24-26 (NLT)

They will speak of the glorious splendor of your majesty, and I will meditate on your wonderful works.

—Ps. 145:5

Meet Me There

Bound for the beach and the open air,
Asking Jesus to meet me there,
In the rising sun and the grains of sand,
As the waves come crashing in to land.

Broken shells washed up on shore,
Shattered, battered, cracked, and scored,
Barely surviving the sea's control;
Only the lucky make it through whole.

The seagulls cry as they search for food,
Hoping a tourist is in a sharing mood.
Men sit on the rocks jutting into the sea,
Casting their lines and feeling so free.

What beautiful castles the children create,
Shaping and sculpting as I sit and wait.
Jesus, sweet Jesus, is on His way
To meet me at the beach today.

Meet Me There

Ever so slowly, as the sun says good-bye
And the moon proudly takes its place in the sky,
Jesus and I sit side by side,
Watching two shooting stars collide.

We marvel together at God's mighty power,
His glorious majesty displayed in each hour.
Closing my eyes and bowing my head,
A humble prayer of thanks is said.

Thus the heavens and the earth were completed in all their vast array. By the seventh day God had finished the work he had been doing; so on the seventh day he rested from all his work. And God blessed the seventh day and made it holy, because on it he rested from all the work of creating that he had done.
—Gen. 2:1-3

Look Around

In all of God's creation,
There is nothing more profound,
Than the love that He's bestowed on us
When we choose to look around.

The heavens are a vast expanse
That twinkles in the night,
And in the day, the morning star
He placed to bring us light.

He formed the earth we live on,
Making water, land, and trees.
The beauty of this landscape
Can bring us to our knees.

Every living creature
Was fashioned by His hand,
Each one uniquely different,
Brought to life at His command.

Look Around

And yet He wasn't finished,
As He paused to take a look.
He wanted something special,
So in His hands some dust He took.

From this dust He formed a man
And breathed life into him.
And made the man a partner
Out of a rib from deep within.

God's given all these things to us,
And He said that it was good.
Let's not take them for granted
But appreciate His wonders as we should!

Every living creature,
All the water, land, and sea
Are part of God's grand masterpiece
That He's given you and me.

We thank You everlasting God
For the wonders that You've shared,
Giving thought to every detail,
In this world that You've prepared.

So each day as we look around,
Let the beauty of God's love
Sink into our five senses,
Giving praise to God above.

When I consider your heavens, the work of your fingers, the moon and the stars, which you have set in place, what is man that you are mindful of him, the son of man that you care for him?
—Ps. 8:3-4

Creation's Gift

When the sun shines down upon my face,
I feel the warmth of Your embrace.

As the wind blows gently through my hair,
I sense Your presence in the air.

When raindrops fall out of the sky,
It may be You having a cry.

When thunder roars and lightning strikes,
I'm reminded of Your power and might.

The seasons come and then they go,
Changing landscapes create the show.

All the day You shine Your light,
Followed by the dark of night.

Always moving, never slow,
Creation's gift for me to know.

I thank You that Your masterpiece
Of perfect love will never cease.

Creation's Gift

Your breath of life is in all things,
Listen to their voices sing.

Birds of air and fish of sea,
Insects, animals, human beings;

I joyfully go about my days,
Following You in all my ways.

You have laid this beauty at my feet,
Only in You am I complete.

Your heart is glad when I rejoice,
And accept Your gift by choice.

> *How beautiful on the mountains are the feet of those who bring good news, who proclaim peace, who bring good tidings, who proclaim salvation, who say to Zion, "Your God reigns!"*
>
> —Isa. 52:7

The Living Masterpiece

When looking at a sandy beach or all the stars at night,
Our eyes are met with wonder at such an awesome sight.

We're led among the forest trees growing tall and strong,
And listen to the many birds that lift their voices in song.

Sitting on a grassy hill, wind blowing gently on our face,
We marvel at the grandeur of this wide and open space.

The tendrils of the sunshine's rays reach their way to earth,
Illuminating all they touch, helping bring forth nature's birth.

A gentle rain falls from the sky, showering the ground,
Washing clean the landscape, rejuvenating all around.

The mountains and the valleys, open fields, and rolling plains,
Add depth and texture to the masterpiece over which our
    great God reigns.

When we walk out of our homes each day, the canvas that we see
Holds ever-changing colors seen in flowers, sky, and trees.

The Living Masterpiece

Storm clouds come and bring forth rain, thunder and
    lightning strike,
Electrifying flashes shoot their display across the skies.

In the midst of all the rain, the sun peaks through the clouds,
A brilliant hue of color drapes the dark sky like a shroud.

The water of the ocean's waves crash upon the sandy shore,
Creating perfect rhythm in our life's harmonious score.

The seasons, always changing as if they are putting on a show,
All for our enjoyment, while through our busy lives we go.

I write this to remind us that there's so much more to see,
If we just take the time to stop and look and allow ourselves to be.

Give praise to our Creator for the splendor of His work,
Taking care to thank Him daily for giving us these perks.

So enjoy the gift, cherish it, and take time to look around,
Lest we never take for granted all the beauty that abounds.

To order additional copies of this book call:
1-877-421-READ (7323)
or please visit our Web site at
www.WinePressbooks.com

If you enjoyed this quality custom-published book,
drop by our Web site for more books and information.

www.winepressgroup.com
"Your partner in custom publishing."